M000080497

Forever Grateful To You: